Why write this book?

The words of the late, great Arthur Ashe informed me:

"Start where you are. Use what you have. Do what you can."
—Arthur Ashe

THE 6R METHOD

TO ENHANCING
EMPLOYEE EXPERIENCE

A METHOD TO IMPROVE EMPLOYEE ENGAGEMENT, INCOME INEQUALITY, AND PROFITABLE GROWTH

GUY MARINI

THE 6R METHOD
Copyright © 2022 Guy Marini

Produced and printed by Stillwater River Publications.
All rights reserved. Written and produced in the
United States of America. This book may not be reproduced
or sold in any form without the expressed, written
permission of the author(s) and publisher.

Visit our website at
www.StillwaterPress.com
for more information.

First Stillwater River Publications Edition

ISBN: 978-1-958217-36-8 (hardcover)
ISBN: 978-1-958217-04-7 (paperback)

1 2 3 4 5 6 7 8 9 10
Written by Guy Marini
Cover Art by Lindsay Whelan
Published by Stillwater River Publications,
Pawtucket, RI, USA.

Names: Marini, Guy, author.
Title: The 6R method to enhancing employee experience :
a method to improve employee engagement, income
inequality, and profitable growth / Guy Marini.
Description: First Stillwater River Publications edition. |
Pawtucket, RI, USA : Stillwater River Publications, [2022]
Identifiers: ISBN: 978-1-958217-04-7
Subjects: LCSH: Leadership. | Employee motivation. |
Personnel management. | Organizational effectiveness.
Classification: LCC: HD57.7 .M37 2022 |
DDC: 658.4/092--dc23

This book is dedicated to the employees of NEPTCO Incorporated who delivered amazing results by believing in each other.

Contents

Foreword

THE TARGET AUDIENCE FOR THIS BOOK is primarily those in senior executive positions at companies that could be classified as middle market and larger. In my mind, a company with 100 employees and revenue of $20 mil or more should be able to consider the management philosophy described herein.

The book is intended to influence those at the vice president, general manager, president, and CEO levels to include those that serve on the board of directors.

Secondly, this writing is intended to speak to middle and senior managers. This level of management is critical to the success of enterprises as these men and women are closer to rank-and-file workers. They know their people (if they are good at what they do) and can sometimes more readily see the value of the ideas described herein and can influence their bosses.

Finally, I hope that those who grind out the actual work of our corporations will take a moment to read this book. They are so critical to the success of the organization at large and must be recognized for what they do. Perhaps one of the things these people need is to understand their true value—this book certainly intends to emphasize this to management at all levels.

If the values of *The Six Rs* are properly implemented and adhered to, your results will improve and the needs of people up and down the organization will be increasingly met as profitability grows and shareholder value is enhanced.

A LITTLE BACKGROUND HISTORY ON NEPTCO: NEPTCO Inc was founded in 1953 principally to produce identification tapes for a variety of markets. Its most well-known products at the time were packaging tapes. One such tape was used by department stores. In those days, a customer's purchases were places in boxes. Those boxes were closed and subsequently secured with a narrow printed decorative tape that identified the name of the department store. (See old movies from the 1950s!) The other well-known product was a narrow printed tape that said "Say It With Flowers." This "flower tape" was used by every florist shop in the US to wrap fresh flowers together at the stems.

The company's core competencies were in fiber handling, adhesive technology, printing, slitting, and winding. A few of the company's customers were producers of wire and cable products. The company's products were used by manufacturers that made cable for the military. Those cables were basically communication cables that had to meet certain military specifications. The identification tape products by NEPTCO identified the company that made the cable and showed the military specification that the cable met.

The company's competencies fit in nicely with the needs of wire and cable companies such as Belden,

AT&T, Commscope, Times Fiber, General Cable, Southwire, and many others. Over time NEPTCO grew its technical capabilities to include laminating, coating, and manufacturing custom glass fiber profiles.

The company experienced steady growth in the '70s, '80s, and '90s as the US telecommunications capability/capacity grew for phone, cable TV, and the internet. Coaxial and fiber optic cables were being installed throughout the US with NEPTCO providing shielding tapes, heat seal films, and identification tapes for the copper cable market, as well as non-metallic strength elements for fiber optic cables. In addition, the company developed a line of pulling tape products known as "Muletape™" to install cables.

Given its core competencies in coating, slitting, and winding, the company also introduced cover tapes in the 1980s for the semiconductor and electronics market.

When I joined the company in 1982, NEPTCO sales were approximately $9 mil. By the time the company was sold to private equity firms in partnership with the company's management team the business was doing $120 mil in revenue, had 600 employees, and was manufacturing materials in three plants in the US, a facility in China, and a plant in France.

I WAS FORTUNATE ENOUGH TO LEAD a 600-person engineered materials company called NEPTCO Incorporated for 25 plus years. I joined the business when it was a private company. It then became part of a British public company before we went back to private ownership as part of a private equity buyout. Through various ownership structures, my colleagues and I developed a culture based on teamwork, collaboration, and employee involvement.

I came to call this method of managing our business *The Six Rs* of Employee Engagement. Together, all of the employees of NEPTCO built a successful, profitable company with its employees at the center and a culture based on relentless continuous improvement. Along the way, I came into contact with many business entities: banks, customers, suppliers, consultants, legal/financial counsel, investors, etc. What I observed in some of those entities and the workforce at large was a general decline in the morale of employees. In addition, the media were and are reporting that workers have a growing cynicism and mistrust towards their employers. I saw our company, NEPTCO, as different— it was.

As I ended my time in the workforce, the chasm between company leaders and its people seems to have widened and something called "income inequality" has become a growing part of our national discourse. The most concerning part of this for me is that many believe politicians, well-meaning as they may or may not be, can fix or legislate the growing disparity in income. This idea is absurd to me. There is only one group that can fix this: business leaders.

The people that run our businesses can correct the problem of income inequality if they have the will and a method. The same can be said about the decreasing level of employee engagement. It can be increased only through the will and leadership of our business hierarchy. All that is needed is the determination to do so and a path to follow.

Through the implementation of *The Six Rs*, businesses can reduce income inequality, build strong bonds with their employees, drive profitable growth, and deliver value to shareholders. Your employees, associates, and colleagues will become one driving force; it all starts with the organization's culture and a method I have defined as *The Six Rs*:

> Respect
> Responsibility
> Recognition
> Reward
> Reciprocity
> Relationships

The 6R Method

Respect
Responsibility
Recognition
Reward
Reciprocity
Relationships

One Practitioner's View

The 6 R Method

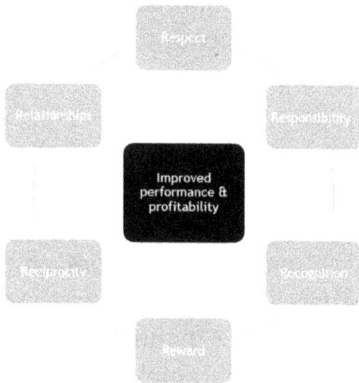

Respect

Relationships

Responsibility

Improved
performance &
profitability

Reciprocity

Recognition

Reward

The 6 R's...© Guy Marini

Chapter 1: The Practitioner's View

THIS BOOK WILL NOT be filled with charts, statistics, and the like. It will consist of the reflections of a multi-year senior executive in a $120 mil plus revenue company who is a self-declared empath and team player.

I came into the leadership of NEPTCO when the founder's family sold the business to a British public company only to have the founder and his two sons retire shortly after the sale. The acquirers looked to fill the position of VP/general manager from inside the company. In 1987 I was chosen to run the company at the ripe old age of 32, having spent five years with the company, four of them as controller.

For that time, the owners had an enlightened view as to my training when I joined the business. I spent very little time in the accounting department in my first 100 days at the company.

I spent time in every department in the company—production, engineering, R & D, purchasing, sales, customer service, and human resources. I worked side by side with machine operators on the production floor so that I could learn firsthand how the company's products were manufactured. I listened as our customer service personnel took customer orders and fielded customer complaints/concerns. I was on sales calls to learn how our products were consumed in our customer operations and was educated as to issues regarding service, competition, and customers' new product needs. I sat in on meetings with critical suppliers and watched our purchasing team negotiate for quality raw materials at an appropriate cost.

Two things happened through this training process: I developed a foundational understanding of the business, and I built relationships in each and every functional area of the business.

In the next few years I was a leader in the efforts to install a fully integrated ERP system and define/implement a company-wide profit improvement program. I also played a critical role in the development of a formal planning process that included the company's first ever strategic plan and company goal setting to include the business unit and functional department's tactical objectives and budgets.

With the help of ownership and our team, the company-wide initiatives I was part of became part of the success story of NEPTCO—my success was grounded in the relationships I was able to build during that initial training as well as my ability to communicate and resolve interpersonal issues without alienating my peers, colleagues, and ownership.

I was recommended for the job as president by the founder of NEPTCO and got the job with one condition: I had one year to prove myself to the new ownership group or I was out. In the years that followed, we grew sales/earnings, improved quality statistics, gained market share, and continued to build employee longevity/loyalty in virtually every plant/department.

I was young, so I worked hard and did a lot of listening and observing. One thing I knew for sure was that if the company and I were to succeed, we would need the effort of our entire team to include my direct reports; those that worked on the factory floor and everyone in between.

What I found in those first few years of leading the business was that our people throughout the organization at many levels had ideas, suggestions, and yes, complaints. They cared more than I thought they would. It was clear to me that they wanted to be part of something bigger than themselves. They wanted to be respected and listened to.

This was eye-opening to me. Why was this eye-opening to me? For a number of years, I heard that our employees were "there for the paycheck." Systems and methods needed to be dumbed down because of the quality of the workforce.

I began to study the problem further and found research that indicated that 67 percent of US workers are not engaged at work.

A Gallup State of the American Workplace Report found:

- 16 percent of US workers are disengaged
- 51 percent of US workers are not engaged, they're just there

Jim Clifton, chairman and CEO of Gallup said: "The old ways no longer achieve the intended results.

Now, why is this?[1]

My thoughts are as follows:

- Employees are micromanaged
- Employees have little or no input into improving product, process, or service
- Communication is woefully inadequate between executive management and the rank and file

---

1   Source— Gallup's State of the Workplace Report, 2015/2016

Finally, I believe from my experience as a practitioner, that growth in company profit is not shared in any meaningful way with the workforce at large. Executives, senior management, and certain others are well taken care of through bonuses, stock option plans, and the rest, but the majority of the workforce . . . well—nope! Not happening.

If you accept some of my observations, is it any wonder employees are not engaged in the workplace?

I'm offering an anecdote here: Hollywood is pretty good at mirroring what's happening in society. I'm not saying that everything that comes out of Hollywood represents what's happening in our culture at large, but when one of Hollywood's successful franchises is *Horrible Bosses* you gotta stop and wonder—why does this connect so well with audiences?

It would appear to me that a lot of people must have run across business leaders who have huge egos, are narcissistic, and behave like self-important "stoonads" as my Italian friends would say.

So . . . okay . . . I get it—but so what?

When employees feel marginalized or disconnected, my belief is that they will work for a while; and then, when they can, they will simply move on. One of the least discussed problems in the workplace is the issue of high turnover.

Turnover drove me crazy. A high turnover rate means lost production, lost revenue, and more stress on the employees who remain in the department. Even our company, which was viewed as employee-friendly, hated to miss productivity and output targets. So this would mean more pressure and overtime for the remaining folks, not to mention time spent acquiring and training new employees.

There are studies that show that jobs earning less than $50k per year are approximately 50 percent of US jobs. These studies indicate that the cost of replacing lost employees amounts to 20 percent of the person's annual compensation. To me, that seems light. I would estimate the cost to be north of 30 percent of the cost of the employee.

In addition, how on earth do you measure the lost input and ideas of the 67 percent of the workforce (as reported by Gallup) that is totally disengaged or just there to collect a paycheck? Think of it this way: what is the value of the lost opportunity to increase profitability due to employee disengagement? Start to imagine the ways your business could increase profitability by simply improving employee engagement.

One of my mentors shared with me something he called the 25-50-25 Rule. I only heard of it once throughout my business career. That gentleman's name was Mr. Peter Farago. Mr. Farago was of Jewish heritage and was captured during World War II, spending some time in a German work camp. He escaped, made his way to America, and was educated at the Rhode Island School of Design. He earned a degree in textile engineering. As he entered the workforce in his adopted country in the 1950s, he was asked by some investors to look at a company called the New

England Printed Tape Company. As Mr. Farago shared in his later years, it was an interesting business with decent technology and a pile of unpaid bills.

Well, under Mr. Farago's leadership, along with his sons' intelligence and the help of some young, bright managers, plus a solid workforce, it didn't stay that way for long. The company became a well-respected supplier in several markets related to communications known for innovation, quality, and excellent service.

One day he was chatting with me about the people in our company and he said, "I believe in the 25-50-25 Rule."[2]

I asked what it was . . .

- 25 percent of your people will buy in to what you are trying to achieve and contribute;

- 50 percent of your people will buy in and contribute if they are engaged in the business, and the only way they'll engage in your business is if they truly feel appreciated and part of something bigger than themselves;

- 25 percent of your people will find it difficult to buy in. You must challenge yourself to help them find a way out of the company so that the rest can drive business improvements.

---

2 A management consultant named John Maxwell talks about the 25-50-25 Principle of Change...Mr. Farago shared his view with me in the early to mid 80s. Mr. Maxwell's views appear much later.

When I asked how one would identify where a person fit in the rule, he shared, "People reveal themselves—you will know." Now as far as I know, there is no empirical evidence or studies to support Mr. Farago's 25-50-25 Rule. However, in my experience, I found that his rule was directionally accurate.

Every time our company was sharing our vision, goals, and operational plans, I knew there were some people we couldn't reach (the bottom 25 percent if you will). I could also feel the zeal from the "Believers"—the top 25 percent. I always tailored the presentation and shared my passion regarding what we were trying to achieve to the middle 50 percent.

I believe, wholeheartedly, that you need to fight for that 50 percent. They are looking for cracks in your argument. They are looking to see if you are going to support your goals/vision with resources. Are you and your leadership team going to put the time and effort into these goals? Are you going to talk about them just once a year? Will there be performance updates? Will there be corrections to the plan if required?

I share this background to provide some context regarding the genesis of *The Six Rs*.

Chapter 2: Income Inequality

THE PEW RESEARCH CENTER SHARES that the gaps between upper-income and middle- to lower-income households are rising; and, the share held by middle-income households is falling. There are many causes of income inequality. The root causes include globalization, union representation decline, the lack of purchasing power provided by the minimum wage, quality/availability of education, improved efficiency due to technology changes, and others. There is a lot of data and debate about income inequality, and opinions are plentiful. The data does seem to indicate that the rich did indeed get richer as we dug out from the 2008 financial crisis. Kimberly Amadeo shares that "between 1993 and 2015, the average family income grew by 25./ percent. The top 1 percent received 52 percent of the growth, 48 percent of the growth was received by the bottom 99 percent."

I don't want to get lost in a mountain of data, selected facts, and some of the hysteria behind the debate.

I believe what is indisputable is that there has been a rise in income inequality. It affects the majority of the workforce negatively. It, of course, affects purchasing power and it also reduces the mobility of the workforce. In addition, growing income inequality can affect choices for healthcare options, availability of quality education, and more. All of this leads to a growing mistrust between business leaders, successful entrepreneurs, and the people who do the day-to-day work in our organizations.

Certain corporate media and politicians use the issue of income inequality to further divide our people. When the politicians enter the fray, they raise certain socialist solutions like a universal basic income. They also clamor for investments in education and training to increase individual wealth opportunity, generally paid for by—yes, you guessed it—higher taxes on those earning more than others. Or, they suggest ending outsourcing to low labor cost countries as a way to bring "good-paying jobs" back to the US. Producing goods here in the US will make them more expensive. The result: another tax of sorts on consumers.

The outsourcing debate is complicated and I am in favor of producing critical US products in the US, and yet outsourcing does have a place in our economic system. Those more enlightened than I can tackle the outsourcing issue.

The investors who risk capital and the innovators are the cornerstones of our very successful economic system, yet in my view, it is incumbent upon them to share their organization's income growth with those that do the work. I am not talking about handouts and giveaways, *I am talking about sharing some of the growth in company-earned income with the folks who show up every day and execute.*

I argue here for sharing growing profits with your employees at all levels that are in service of the company's mission and vision. There are many profit-sharing systems that include quarterly/annual bonus methods that should and must extend throughout your organization. Let us as business leaders leave the politicians on the sidelines and begin a cause to share a part of the growth in corporate profits with our employees. Nothing really stands in our way of doing this. The company must use its growth in profits to fund needed capital spending, research development, and the like, AND provide additional compensation for its people. We must find a way to do this; it will improve the financial strength of our people and their families, and will help them find higher quality education for their children and better health care, which everyone should have a shot at.

This belief is rooted in the work ethic that made the US the strongest economy in the world and established us as the leading country in the free world, a country that still attracts immigrants searching for a better life. I am not against successful business leaders, entrepreneurs, and investors making a lot of money. I simply believe that as corporate profits grow it is sound economic and moral policy to make sure that those who do the work share in the benefits.

I see the other choice as, let the politicians fix it. Yikes! Can you imagine?

The income inequality issue is complex, and I believe politicians cannot solve it. I do believe politicians could adopt the philosophy expressed here and use their particular bully pulpit to encourage businessmen to do better.

Businesses don't do this today because of, yes, greed. Of course, one of the guiding principles for business is to pay as little as possible for all costs to improve earnings, satisfy shareholders, and maximize bonus/incentive opportunities. No big revelation there. However, due to tremendous improvements in productivity through technology, the nature of work itself has changed. The result is compensation has not kept up with rising costs. People at lower and middle income levels are getting more and more squeezed.

Our political process does generate favorable programs for workers, such as family leave, and worker safety through OSHA. However, when government attempts something massive like health care, the results are less than acceptable. The Affordable Health Care Act, a noble attempt to provide low-cost alternatives for those lacking proper health care, costs on average $328 to $482 per month. Is this affordable to lower income earners?! There are tax credits which people can obtain if they meet certain requirements related to federal poverty levels. Anecdotally, I have spoken to people who use the Affordable Care Act and their experience is not generally positive.

Therefore, in my view, how can politicians, either at the state or federal level, legislate a way to combat

income inequality over so many different indus-
tries with companies facing ever changing competition (global and local), environmental challenges,
tax issues, etc., etc., etc.? It's mind-boggling to even
consider where and how to start.

I, therefore, conclude that the method described
in *The Six Rs* is a commonsense, local, straightfor-
ward and emotionally intelligent approach. I remain
in close contact with many people who own or
lead businesses. One of the business challenges they
consistently speak of is the inability to attract and/or
retain people. I find many of these conversations to be
a mile long and an inch deep.

With so many issues facing company presidents,
CEOs, and boards, ideas like *The Six Rs* expressed
herein seldom get a hearing.

I believe this is an opportune time for business
leaders to stop and consider *The Six Rs* as poten-
tial guiding values. I believe many who read this
material can agree that it's important to respect
your workforce, give them the tools to be responsible, recognize them, etc.

However, when it comes to reward and sharing
the growth in earnings with employees, my generation
of presidents, CEOs, etc., may find it foreign, not digest-
ible, the words of a dreamer. Some in my generation
may and do embrace this notion in some fashion. I truly
believe the generation of managers/leaders who are
now coming into positions of authority will ultimately

embrace these ideas fully. My hope, trust, and challenge is with them—people, please figure out a way to do this!

You want full engagement with your employees/colleagues/associates, then take the guiding principles of *The Six Rs* and include sharing the growth in earnings with your people. I predict you will unleash the full power of the human spirit as embodied by the work ethic that is the foundation of the American Dream.

Or . . . we can go along this current path we are on, and watch our society deteriorate as income gaps grow. We can watch the people who are at the lower end of the pay scale get demoralized and resentful. We are beginning to see the cracks and fissures in our society today. It is not pretty. A key aspect— maybe one of the most important aspects—of the American system is that it provides upward mobility. If the income disparity between the top executives and the rank and file continues to grow, I believe our country will change in a way we will regret.

The vision for our business leaders must include a method to reduce income inequality and improve employee engagement while achieving profitable, sustainable growth.

I believe there is a path forward in the management method I have labeled "*The Six Rs.*"

The Six Rs of Employee Sustainability:

A method to improve employee engagement, income inequality, and profitable growth.

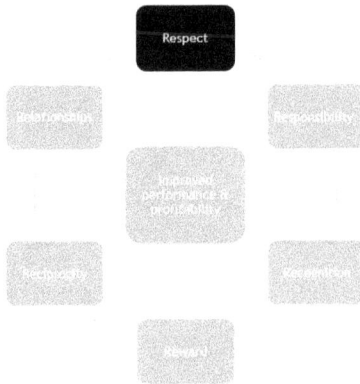

The 6 R Method

Respect

Relationship

Responsibility

Improved performance & profitability

Reciprocity

Recognition

Reward

The 6 R's...© Guy Marin

Chapter 3: Respect

DATA SHOWS THAT 67 PERCENT of US workers don't feel respected in the workplace. Said another way, many workers leave companies because they feel underappreciated and undervalued.

The data is worse for millennials—for them, being appreciated and respected by their peers and management is an absolute. As many as 8 of 10 share that they would leave their place of employment if they felt undervalued.

I am in my mid-60s and have seen many a company that views its people as replaceable parts. It manifests itself in an upper management attitude that says, "Hey if you don't like it here, it's okay—you can leave." I see this in some of the leaders of my generation and those that are a bit older. I used to think that as my and older generations moved on into retirement that things would change. I'm not sure they have.

It's amazing to me that two-thirds of our people don't feel respected. I was raised to respect others, including peers, colleagues, and those that worked for me. One of my mentors who recommended me for the leadership position at NEPTCO shared that I would listen and be respectful of our board of directors, as well as those on the factory floor. This was the greatest compliment I ever received.

I don't believe that people go to work every day thinking, "Hey, I'm going to do lousy work today!" I believe in the implicit dignity of a human being. I have been wrong from time to time, yet I remain steadfast in this belief.

To me, it's pretty simple.

Respect in the workplace means:

- Listening to your people's concerns; and then, do your best to address them.
- Treat your people how you want to be treated.

One way we showed people we cared was by conducting anonymous employee surveys on a biannual basis. These employee surveys became popular to spot union activity in non-union shops many years ago. We used them to highlight where we, as management, were doing well and where we needed to improve.

We implemented a feedback system—we shared the survey findings (withholding confidential disclosures and people's names, of course) with our employee population. Then, together with HR and managers, we created company-wide and department-specific goals to work on areas of needed improvement. Now we didn't get everything right, but our people recognized the effort, the seriousness of our follow-up, and the method we developed to address their issues.

Another thing I began to do was periodically ask simple questions. I would get 600 index cards for our 600 employees and ask them a question. I handed the cards out at employee meetings. One of the questions was the following: "If you could make one suggestion to improve the company, what would it be?" I did set some basic ground rules like, "Please don't respond by suggesting 'fire Marini' " (of course, some people did).

I asked people to focus on sales initiatives, new product ideas, process improvement thoughts, methods to improve teamwork, etc. Most people complied . . . of course others (think the bottom 25 percent from the 25-50-25 Rule) couldn't resist the opportunity to speak directly to me about their gripes, despite me telling them that this was not the forum for that. Yet, some of their issues resonated with me.

My assistant and I compiled the info—just my assistant and me. I would categorize the responses and share the input with my leadership team.

I was always amazed by the responses. Our people provided thoughtful, positive ideas. The impressive part of it for me was the passion they expressed. They cared—they liked the fact that there was no filter between them and me.

I gave them feedback based on their input—some of their input made it into the annual operating plans. What I found was this simple act of asking for their thoughts and ideas built respect in my relationships with our workforce, and resulted in me respecting our people more.

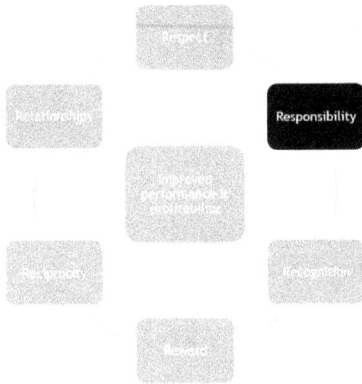

Chapter 4: Responsibility

WORK RESPONSIBILITY CAN BE DEFINED AS FOLLOWS:

> *Work responsibility refers to the degree to which your workers comprehend their jobs and how their specific job functions contribute to the success of the operation.*

It is an absolute requirement of the employees and those in managerial/leadership roles to make those responsibilities known to their workers.

In the absence of well-defined responsibilities in the workplace, managers tend to micromanage. This

despised managerial behavior leads to job dissatis-
faction, conflict, lost productivity, and deteriora-
tion of morale.

It's clear that managers must develop accurate,
clear, and specific job descriptions. These job
descriptions need periodic scrutiny and must be
challenged from time to time. My experience is
that some companies job describe in a way that
dooms the employee to failure. The most frequent
issue I have seen is where a person at a certain level
is "job described" to perform at a level not consistent with the actual job but represents some manager's wish list as to what he/she hopes the employee
can accomplish. For example, one can't expect a
maintenance worker capable of troubleshooting or
fixing machines to be a design engineer of equipment. Granted, with training, education, and experience, one can grow, but job descriptions need to be
matched with the compensation and skill level of
the person so as not to frustrate the employee and
company management.

Another case where I believe most companies can
improve is in training. Taking the time to train your
new people is critical to the employees' success and
that of the company. Companies need to take into
account how the newly hired individual learns—
some do great with classroom-type training, others
need to actually learn on the job with proper super-
vision from a manager or a person skilled in the job
function. I believe in refresher training for the newly
hired employee. This refresher training has to occur

within a specific time period of the hiring date, say 60-90 days from the hire date. This will reveal the newly hired individual's understanding of the job and any bad habits or workarounds the person may have come up with to complete certain job duties. Annual certification or refresher training must be considered as well. Many companies also use refresher training to remind people of safety protocols.

The way for a company to avoid the age-old trap of micromanaging is to build control parameters for processes/products/services. In the manufacturing world, this is commonly referred to as standards: throughput per machine and man-hour, raw material yields, etc. In the administrative environment, many if not most activities can and should have expectations for "production." The number of calls for customer service per day, the number of invoices processed by billing, the time required to process/ submit payroll, etc.

In my later years as a practitioner, I saw more and more metrics for performance being introduced in administrative departments. Accurate job descriptions, proper training, and measurable performance standards will lead your workers to do their jobs well. If your workers do their jobs without being micromanaged, you will find that this will improve accountability and they will be answerable for their workplace performance. Employee engagement and satisfaction will improve. Employees will find that they are trusted to do their job versus having to suffer a micromanager who rides them.

The Six Rs—Responsibility
Empower your people to <u>own</u> their jobs

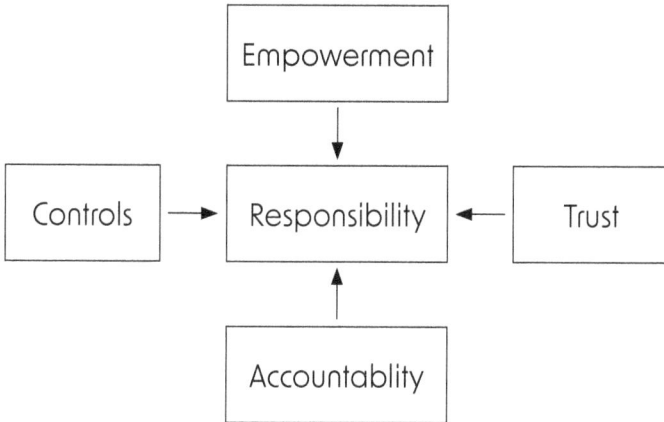

```
                  ┌──────────────────┐
                  │   Empowerment    │
                  └──────────────────┘
                            │
                            ▼
┌───────────┐     ┌──────────────────┐     ┌───────────┐
│ Controls  │ ──▶ │  Responsibility  │ ◀── │   Trust   │
└───────────┘     └──────────────────┘     └───────────┘
                            ▲
                            │
                  ┌──────────────────┐
                  │  Accountablity   │
                  └──────────────────┘
```

Management's job is to monitor and direct positive corrective action when certain performance parameters are not met. Corrective action done with those doing the job, others that provide input into the job process, and the "customers" of the job's output will provide context, identify root causes, and allow the team involved to craft fixes and correction action. Once problem-solving methods like the one described are implemented, the entire system being studied will improve as will teamwork and collaboration.

The 6 R Method

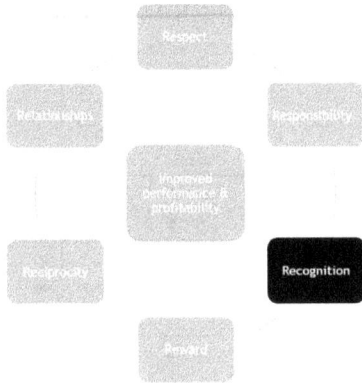

The 6 R's...© Guy Mar⬛

Chapter 5: Recognition

EMPLOYEE RECOGNITION IS USUALLY DEFINED as the open acknowledgment and expressed appreciation for employees' contributions to the workplace.

In my view, the key to recognition is to reinforce the behaviors you want to see more of. Our management team used recognition to improve teamwork; build success in identifying, designing, and manufacturing new products; improve process yields; provide excellent customer service; and much more. We've even recognized those that take their time to consistently and effectively recognize others.

Here are a few outcomes you can expect:

- Employees that look forward to coming to work because they are held in high esteem by their peers and management.
- Improved employee loyalty and retention.
- Increased likelihood that your people will participate in corrective action teams and other company initiatives.

You will also observe an *increase in morale*. When a new employee is onboarded, his/her new fellow employees will let the new hire know what kind of a company they've joined. Your people will spread the word in the community—at church, local youth sports leagues, and other social groups—that your company is a good place to work.

Here are some examples of what we did to recognize people, improve company morale, and increase employee retention:

- A face-to-face expression of thanks: The best and purest method, especially if you are properly informed of the person's work accomplishments and you are genuine.
- A handwritten thank-you note: Written by *you*, not your assistant. Some of the greatest business leaders utilized this practice— utilized may be the wrong word; they made

time to do this. In a medium-sized company like mine (600 people at the high point), it wasn't hard to do, especially because I made it a priority to get the proper information sent to me so I could express my appreciation.

- A simple phone call to say thank you: Your people can hear your voice, and your tone. They will discern your sincerity. The reward for you is threefold: you are doing the right thing; those that you recognize will tell you how much they appreciate it; they will proudly tell their family that they were recognized by a senior person.

RECOGNITION CEREMONIES

Set up a process where people can be recognized by their peers. Yes, you have to be careful that people don't simply recognize their friends, but that becomes very clear over time. While you may make some mistakes along the way, you can clean that up. Our recognition ceremonies were funded in our annual budgets and included lunch on the company and gifts: tickets to the movies, restaurant gift certificates, gift certificates to big box stores, etc. Tailor your recognition award to the specific locale. In Rhode Island, movie theater tickets and restaurant gift certificates were popular. In North Carolina, people preferred gift cards to Cabela's, Walmart, and restaurants—well, everyone loves to eat!

So in our case, a group of 40-50 people would gather. You could not imagine the lift this gave our people and the fun we had. The leader of the recognition group would read the nomination that included what the person or a group of people did. You would see nods around the room. The person being recognized would smile, sometimes blush, etc., and walk up to receive their award and applause from their peers. Powerful . . . absolutely powerful. Everyone in that group—recognized or not—knew they worked with and for a group of people who cared.

CELEBRATORY LUNCHES

Bring your team together to celebrate a record month, the achievement of a significant milestone in a company-wide project, successfully landing a new customer, etc. As senior executives, take the time to attend these luncheons; don't just stay with the group you're most comfortable with or see the most. Get to know more of your people in a relaxed, celebratory environment.

Find a way to celebrate work anniversaries—gifts should be provided at 5, 10, 15, 20, 25 years, etc. If you want people to stay with your company, simply recognize their work anniversaries!

There are endless, relatively simple methods to recognize your people.

Peter and Adam Chase of Chase Corporation led the acquisition of NEPTCO Incorporated which was finalized in late June of 2012. Chase Corporation integrated NEPTCO into Chase carefully, methodically, and successfully. Chase Corporation adopted some of NEPTCO's recognition programs and modified them to fit Chase's human resource beliefs/systems. I was delighted to see this happen.

Finally—and this is directed at senior executives—what does it mean to you to have a peer, a member of your board of directors or someone else in authority, recognize your accomplishments? It feels pretty good, doesn't it?

The 6 R Method

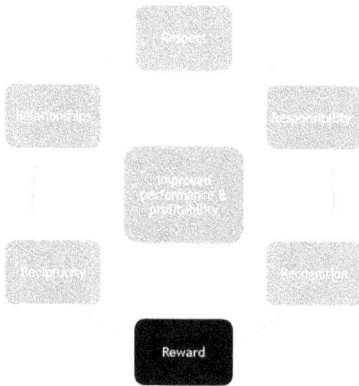

The 6 R's...© Guy Marini

Chapter 6: Reward

REWARD IS SIMPLY DEFINED as "compensating a person for service, merit, or achievements."

Service. Merit. Achievement.

Service in this context, to me means doing the grind of the job day in and day out. Pretty simple.

Merit implies something earned, honorable; i.e., giving of oneself to accomplish something that is better than expected. Greater than the norm.

Achievement to me is the accomplishment of the goal, the vision. The objective that when set is usually the decision of those at the upper ends of the organi-zation. When the objective is delivered to those challenged to meet it, the objective is sometimes met with some derision. Yet, in my experience, as a practitioner and member of the team, oftentimes the team delivers service, merit, and achievement. When people earn merit and strive to meet the objective that the organization sets, then those people—*all* of those people—should be rewarded.

The sharing of the financial fruits of the company has become lopsided in my view. Again, from my perch as a business leader, practitioner, and one who came up through the ranks.

The rest of this chapter is a simple reimagining of one element of our reward structure. It's not a whole-sale reimagining, it's simply an adjustment to the existing structure that, I believe, is part of the solution to growing income inequality.

Step back as you consider the thesis or thoughts provided herein. Let's remember that a cornerstone of the American experience is upward mobility. The opportunity to improve one's lot in life is the defining characteristic of our collective experience that must continue. Or, in my view, the success of the American experience/culture will diminish and this will threaten the future success of the American experiment.

Let's look at our reward structure and begin to deal with income inequality. The power of our businesses and Corporate America is huge—rather than wait for well-meaning politicians and their influencers to solve this problem, let's do it ourselves.

First, fair pay commensurate with the job at hand. Competitive and complete benefits are table stakes. Your local market for labor and industry standards will largely dictate your basic compensation package. Not paying enough, below average benefits, the quality and turnover of your workers will tell the story. I am not saying that where we are regarding the pay and benefits our corporations offer in general is great. I will leave that argument to others as that is not the main focus of this work.

I believe companies need to measure what income inequality looks like in their organizations. Measure your organization's income disparity between executive/senior management and the so-called rank and file. Does the CEO make 20, 30, 40, or 50 times more than the average worker? More than 50 times? How about senior management?

There is also available data regarding a "living wage," i.e. a wage high enough to maintain a normal standard of living. Measure your organization's wage/benefits package against the available data regarding a living wage. The information *is* available. Work the numbers so that you can understand if there is an issue.

I acknowledge that there are many variables involved with compensation and reward systems, including the size of your business and so many others, but let's dive in!

My concern as a practitioner is that we need to start somewhere as business leaders or the solutions will come from Washington D.C.—that terrifies me. So here's the central thesis of *The Six Rs* regarding reward and reducing income inequality:

Share growing profits with your employees that are in service of the company's mission and vision at all levels.

Simply stated: no growth in earnings means there is nothing to share. As I follow corporate earnings in general, it seems there has been significant growth in the earnings of middle-market and large companies. The business press and social media is filled with stories of bonuses, stock packages, and the rest driving the compensation of senior management higher and higher. I have experience in the middle market and I've seen and experienced it firsthand. What is wrong with sharing some of the growth in earnings with those at the lower income levels?

I can hear the arguments now . . . innovators, senior people, investors, and others take the risks and are removed when targets aren't hit; and, therefore must have the higher reward. No argument; but, again . . . what about those people that execute the plan, day in and day out?

I ran a medium-sized manufacturing company. My executive team, our top level managers, and I could come up with the best strategies, operational plans, and tactics, but if the workers in the factory couldn't execute product quality, timeliness in deliveries, etc., it was all for naught.

There are so many profit-sharing systems that include quarterly/annual bonus methods—we need to come up with something that extends throughout the organization. This is not a quasi-socialist rant. I am talking about the company's earned income and sharing some of the growth in earned income with the people who execute day in and day out.

The beliefs I'm sharing are not intended to be a down-to-the-last-detail cookbook on how to do this. My intention is to provide a thought-provoking idea for business leaders.

Imagine a $100 mil manufacturing business producing engineered parts for the military and aerospace industries that earns 22.5 percent EBITDA and has experienced year over year growth in earned income.

So this sounds like a nice medium-sized profitable business . . .

Let's assume the company requires some of the EBITDA for new capital equipment, upgrades to machinery/building, and improvements to IT systems. The company will have to pay its taxes. The company may have some debt to service, and it may wish to pay some dividends to the shareholders that put their capital at risk. It might look like something like this:

EBITDA	$22,500,000
Less: Depreciation	(2,000,00)
: Interest Expense	(1,750,000)
Operating Income	18,750,00
Taxes @ 30%	(5,625,000)
Income After Taxes	$13,125,000
Less: Cash Requirements	
Equipment and IT	(2,500,000)
Debt Service	(1,250,000)
Dividends	(1,000,000)
Available Cash Flow	$8,375,000

Now let's assume we buy into this Six Rs philosophy:

A $100 mil revenue company should have, from my experience, about 500 people working in the business. That would say that revenue per person is about $200,000. This is generally indicative that the business is reasonably healthy.

Now, let's assume that 50 people in the organization are eligible to participate in some kind of bonus plan . . . executives, sales people, department managers, plant managers, technical professionals, etc. The company's had a good year and these people have received their bonus and the cost of those bonuses have already been deducted from earnings. Good for those folks! This, however, leaves 450 people out of the bonus pool.

So we as senior management, newly informed by *The Six Rs* (just go with me on this) decide to reserve 20 percent of $8.375 mil of available cash flow for the rank and file. That would be roughly $1.675 mil. Therefore if we share $1.675 mil amongst 450 people, each person, on average, would be eligible for a $3,722 bonus.

Assuming the average person in the company outside of the executives, senior management, and certain professional staff make $40,000, a $3,722 bonus would be 9.3 percent of base pay. Let's also assume that the average person received a 3 percent annual pay raise. A 3 percent annual increase ($1,200) coupled with a $3,722 bonus per this exercise would mean that the person making $40,000 received a 12.3 percent increase in compensation year over year, or $4,922 in total.

If in the following year this mythical company were to fall back to $18 mil in EBITDA, then there would be no growth in EBITDA and therefore no "fruit" to be shared throughout the organization for that particular fiscal year.

The other thing to consider is the net cost of what I'll call the "income inequality bonus" to the company after taxes.

Let's assume an all-in tax rate of 30 percent per the previous example. The company discussed that earned $16.75 mil of operating income had a tax bill of $5.625 mil. Now, we assume this same company agreed to pay its employees a share of the growing profits through the "Income Inequality Bonus."

Let's take a look at the "new" tax bill:

Operating Income	$18,750,000
Loss: "Income Inequality Bonus"	1,675,000
Revised Operating Income	17,075,000
Taxes @ 30%	5,122,500

The company would have paid $5.625 mil in taxes if it did not pay the "Income Inequality Bonus." It now pays $5.123 mil in taxes or a savings of $502k in taxes. Therefore, the financial folks would say the cost of the bonus to the company is actually $1.173 mil vs. $1.675 mil.

Let me ask—would you rather pay the people working in the business to make your company successful something extra, or Uncle Sam and his growing family in state governments?

I believe the answer is obvious. Paying your people a portion of the growing profit makes economic sense AND will drive improved employee engagement, loyalty, and teamwork.

A committed workforce that is respected, made responsible for their jobs, recognized along the journey, and rewarded, will drive sustainable growth. You will have a workforce more devoted to achieving the company's aims.

I strongly believe something like what is suggested herein finally starts to close the income inequality gap. An amount like $4,922 also means a lot to those making $40k per year. It's significant. Is it a ton of money? No. Could more be done in this simple example? Yes. The point is that something needs to change in how we compensate people to deal with growing income inequality.

I am not arrogant or dumb enough to think that this is the only idea that can work. I hope that this illustration and discussion is a starting point for those who understand the points made herein and wish to be part of the solution to growing income inequality.

Business leaders must do something to narrow the income inequality gap. This is something tangible, real, and, very importantly, is not a government giveaway paid for by borrowing money from China and the rest of the world and increasing our national debt.

The 6 R's...© Guy Marr

Chapter 7: Reciprocity

RECIPROCITY IS DEFINED as a mutual giving or receiving. I was honored and had the privilege of leading a great bunch of people. We evolved from a family-owned business with a relatively young management team to a more mature business with experience in different kinds of ownership to include private, public,[3] and private equity ownership. During this period, we wanted to build an inclusive team that recognized and respected all of its people.

We did some great things in the process and we made some mistakes for sure.

---

3 NEPTCO was owned by a British Publicly Owned Company from 1988 to 2000

On the whole, we were successful with respect to our desire to provide all of our workers a place to work where they felt respected. We embarked on a company-wide quality improvement system with periodic follow-up training that gave us a common language to identify and correct problems.

Our recognition systems generally won support from all types of ownership. This included peer-to-peer recognition and manager-to-worker recognition. We also introduced a tier bonus system where a manager was given budgeted dollars to spend on their employees who successfully demonstrated the behaviors the company identified as positive. It wasn't a lot of money but it was a way to say thank you to someone for identifying a problem, working to solve a problem, collaborating with a supplier to improve the quality of raw materials, etc. These tier bonuses were given when the employee did something positive. It was immediate—a person didn't have to wait 'til annual review time to receive some recognition and reward.

In addition, we gave out safety awards, length of service awards, and we publicized people's accomplishments in company newsletters.

Our compensation system was at market but we weren't the highest payer or the lowest. Our benefits were at market, and again, we weren't the highest or lowest. We introduced and implemented achievable bonus systems to include a profit-sharing plan that paid into employees' retirement accounts.

In the end, we did a good job overall, and I believe we did okay on the income inequality front. In retrospect, I wish we had done more.

I'm sharing this because in my experience, as a practitioner, I found that as we became a more employee-centric company, our people responded in kind and did more than expected. This resulted in our people becoming more successful in their work lives. Our people felt good about coming to work. Our ownership groups were satisfied with our results and the returns we generated. We achieved "reciprocity."

I have many memories of what occurred during customer visits. I would always introduce customers to our employees on the factory floor. Our employees always handled themselves with great dignity, showed pride in their work and expressed appreciation for the customer's business. More than once I had customers look at me, basically in amazement, and say "These people really like working here." The care we showed our people came back to us tenfold.

Our management system, now defined as *The Six Rs*, made the company more prosperous. Our company managers routinely received ideas for process improvements, ways to increase product yields, concepts to improve customer satisfaction, and more from our workforce.

I firmly believe that the successful understanding and implementation of *The Six Rs* increases the likelihood of success for your company and once implemented, it's a self-perpetuating process; i.e., reciprocity achieved. You simply need to manage the receipt of your people's input and communicate with them—help them understand why you chose to implement an idea or not. The time and dollars you spend devoting to and implementing *The Six Rs* will come back to you many, many, many times over.

One last point: *The Six Rs* is your management team's responsibility to implement—it's not Human Resources that owns or runs it. The HR team plays a role but you, your managers, and supervisors need to own it.

The 6 R Method

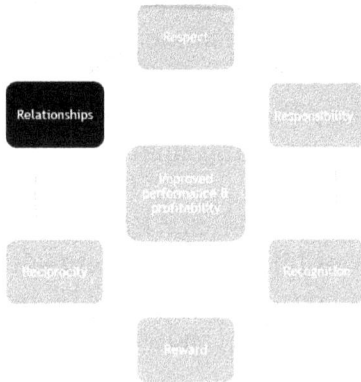

The 6 R's...© Guy Mar

Chapter 8: Relationships

SUCCESSFUL IMPLEMENTATION OF *THE SIX RS* improves relationships across the company.

You will observe:

- Cross-functional teams working more effectively
- Information flowing more quickly and easily up and down the business
- People who feel more cared for caring more about the company and its success

Most organizations fight the silo syndrome, aka, "my team is great—yours . . . not so good." In a manufacturing operation, salespeople sometimes find their operations people inflexible, stubborn, and unwilling to serve the customer. Operations find that salespeople lack an understanding of the process operating parameters of the business, and, therefore, make unreasonable promises to customers. All of this can lead to email bombs and firing verbal missiles at one another.

With a common language to identify and correct problems and the foundation of respect and responsibility supported by senior management, those walls that define the silo syndrome slowly break down. Problem-solving by cross-functional teams becomes the norm, not the exception. It's not a panacea for sure, but I have experienced relationship improvement up and down and across the organization.

Customers and suppliers who get to know your business will notice as well. Customers will provide you the opportunity to service them. Customers will find that if there is a problem to be solved, it will be, because your company's team has evolved and puts the customer's needs over senseless, internal turf battles.

As a 25-year plus practitioner, the relationships we built throughout this process of implementing what I now call *The Six Rs* was our ultimate reward.

As you approach your later years, you will recall with pride the accomplishments of your team and business. You'll also reflect on what could have been regarding those projects, goals that just didn't quite happen. Yet the most treasured of all the experiences are the relationships you built inside the company.

When I left the business I would routinely run into hourly workers, professional staff, and senior managers.

Our interactions were and continue to be sacred to me. At all levels, my colleagues would routinely point to our company as a family. I would ask them what they meant. "A family?" The response was fairly consistent. "The company—you guys—cared for us and in turn, we did our best to get the job done so we could secure all of our jobs and succeed." Some would good-naturedly talk about the tough times, when business wasn't good or we couldn't get our management, sales, or manufacturing process just right, but they substantively all expressed their love—yes love—for the business and their pride in the role they played in its success.

Those talks would usually end with a firm, thoughtful handshake or a hug. For me, those moments—those relationships—are the ultimate reward of my work career. My colleagues and I were part of something that was successful, and therefore we were part of something bigger than ourselves.

The 6 R Method

The 6 R's...© Guy Marini

Chapter 9: Extreme Communication

EXTREME COMMUNICATION IS INTEGRAL to the proper implementation of *The Six Rs*. Senior executives and upper management time and focus need to be constantly challenged. There are many issues and needs of the business that pull on the people at senior levels. Achieving sustainable profitable growth is tantamount. A critical component of achieving sustainable, profitable growth is around us every day; i.e., the people who work in our organization are our most critical assets. How we manage, how we lead, how we communicate; it matters, especially for a process like *The Six Rs* to be successful. Managers, supervisors, lead people, and informal leaders must buy in. For them to buy in, you must provide thoughtful and genuine communication to the organization at large.

Again, as a practitioner, I spent a significant amount of my time preparing for and standing in front of 600 people in groups of 40 to 50 delivering a 30 to 40 minute address. We allowed time for questions which generally ran 20 minutes or so. We scheduled those meetings around lunchtime or shift breaks and provided refreshments, coffee, donuts, lunch, or a light dinner depending on the day, time, and location.

Standing there presenting, I always felt the presence of the 25-50-25 Rule. There were always those who were happy to get paid while listening to me blather on while wondering what we were serving for lunch; i.e. the bottom 25 percent. There were those people who paid attention and "bought into" the presentation; i.e. top 25 percent. Then there were the 50 percent we were fighting to keep motivated. The "State of the Company Talks," as we used to call them, were tailored to the audience. We updated the team briefly on last year's or last quarter's performance and we focused on upcoming goals and what the challenges were. We always shared the role of the employee/department being addressed on what they needed to do to get us where we wanted to go. We also annually provided an update on benefit changes, expected salary increases, etc. Many of our people expressed their thanks for taking the time to simply speak to them. Some employees would approach after lunch to ask a specific question. For those questions that we weren't able to answer on the spot, the local HR person would work with me and the local manager/department leaders to get back to them.

Let's talk about communication during the tough times. Of course, everyone could see when the business was struggling. I recall two specific times: the burst of the internet bubble in 2001, and the financial collapse of 2008. In both cases, like so many businesses, we took action. We did lay off hourly employees due to the lack of work . . . only after we had those people clean and paint the facilities; i.e., we tried to buy time, hoping the business would rebound before having to let people go. The decision to move on from long tenured colleagues was among the most difficult of all. These people were generally longtime contributors with deep knowledge of the business and that particular department. The options we examined were reduced hours, less challenging jobs with lower compensation, etc. These options, in my mind, were demeaning.

The path generally chosen was to discuss the situation with the affected people discreetly and with compassion. We allowed for a flexible timetable; i.e., we didn't pick a day when all the bad news would happen all at once for long term affected colleagues. These people were encouraged to resign with as much honor as possible. Moving on from long tenured colleagues is never easy and whatever you do is never, ever perfect.

Our governing principle was to treat the affected people with dignity. My sense and strong belief is that those who left and those who remained, ultimately respected this approach.

We did not do massive cuts. Rather, we cut salaries by a percentage, reduced discretionary spending, and cut benefits in a measured and careful way. Our message was, "We're in this together"—we didn't want to cut muscle, and while a lot of companies say that, we honestly didn't. I will never forget those meetings standing in front of our people describing what we had to do. No one and I mean no one was happy, but they understood and, ultimately, they respected the approach. Some did not, for sure—"You guys should have cut more people and left our salaries/benefits alone." However, it was not a constant refrain—tacitly, if not openly, they agreed because they came in every day as we worked together to dig ourselves out of the hole. Some people left the company, but only a few. As soon as we could, we restored salaries and benefits. I credit the behavior that our associates demonstrated to our Six Rs philosophy and "extreme communication."

I call it extreme communication because when I met my peers outside of the company—fellow presidents, CEOs of customers, suppliers, and partners—I would ask them about their communication methods. Few resembled our method.

Finally, a simple game plan to get started: At the beginning of the year, set goals and expectations—clearly communicate them to employees. The definition and the effectiveness of communication is measured by "what is heard." So understand who your audience is and tailor the message to the audience. Check back at regular intervals including year-end and share with your people how things are going. Communicate where we have succeeded, also share where we have fallen short without pointing fingers. Depending on the size of your organization, you can do this monthly, quarterly, or semiannually (however I do believe semiannually is not often enough). As your organization grows, script your senior/local managers to deliver the message. Doing this can and will improve alignment in your management team and workforce at large. I was a practitioner pre-Zoom and pre-pandemic. Today, with the available technology, this practice of extreme communication can be done in less time and reach a wider audience.

Chapter 10: Make Time for Fun

I F I HAD THOUGHT OF IT we could have had a seventh R for Recreation, but it really wasn't recreation. As part of our journey through *The Six Rs*, we made time for fun. When we were going through our quality improvement training, we had something called Zero Defects Day, or ZD Day. We never got to zero defects but we celebrated the journey. One of the most memorable ZD Days we had involved a dunk tank! Our senior team, including me, got dunked a hundred times that day—it was a blast.

Our recognition ceremonies were tailored to the location as to the actual awards, but they all were centered around achievement and fun. What I remember about those award ceremonies was not who got the award but the smiles on everyone's faces.

We had annual employee recognition banquets where a local leader or one of our executive team members gave a talk. We gave awards for safety, length of service, etc. The highlight of the employee recognition banquet was the Employee of the Year Award.

People in each of our locations nominated/voted for a person who was admired and respected in the location/department for their contributions to the business, a peer-driven award. I can still feel the location erupt in applause when the presenter would slowly reveal the characteristics and accomplishments of the person . . . and then, finally, the person was announced to cheers and a standing ovation. There was so much power in that moment. The location employee of the year was selected by his/her peers—not management—the highest performer was lauded and given a gift from the company. The best part was that that person would go home from work and share the award proudly with their family.

At our company picnics or other gatherings, the spouse, significant others, and older children would thank us for being the kind of company that allowed for that kind of recognition for an hourly worker, a maintenance person, a customer service representative, etc. The Employee of the Year Award, given the way we did it, was very powerful recognition.

We also did skits to emphasize a goal or objective or to just have fun. In a pressure-filled workplace, making time for fun needs to be a priority. One of our managers, Mr. George Shanahan, materials manager, did an amazing impersonation of a Saturday Night Live character, Father Guido Sarducci. George became "Father Guido Shanahan." He and I would do skits together about something happening in the business. People still talk to me about it when I see them. Father Guido Shanahan and I always delivered some message with Father Guido Shanahan often cleverly off-script and me playing his straight man. George had people laughing with tears in their eyes. You gotta have some fun at work. I found you can have some fun and deliver a message about the business in a lighthearted way.

Chapter 11: Brief Overview—NEPTCO Incorporated

NEPTCO Incorporated 1955-2012

NEPTCO INC. WAS FOUNDED as the New England Print Tape Company in the mid-1950s. It was founded as a decorative ribbon and tape manufacturing business. Shopping, back when the dinosaurs roamed the earth in the 1950s (only kidding), was different. When you went shopping at a department store, your boxes of goods or bundles were wrapped up and tied by a printed tape that identified the name of the store.

The company's most famous of products back then was a narrow printed tape, green at the edges and white in the center that said: "Say It With Flowers." When you bought a bouquet of flowers in the 1950s, the flowers were held together by that tape—seems quaint now . . .

The company struggled for a few years until the owners/investors brought in a textile engineer, a recent graduate of the Rhode Island School of Design named Peter Farago. Mr. Farago bought the business and ultimately, with the help of his sons,

Alan and Paul, that young management team, and a group of solid employees, transformed the business into a supplier of engineered materials to the wire and cable business. Mr. Farago was a wonderful man that was loved by many. Mr. Farago sold the business to a British public company in 1987 when the company had revenue of approximately $35 mil. Shortly thereafter his talented sons left the business as well.

The British public company, Cookson Group PLC, chose me to be VP/general manager in 1988. I was fortunate to work with an extremely dedicated group of people and together we built NEPTCO into a $120 mil plus revenue business with approximately 600 people at its height.

The management team post-1980 were largely what Mr. Farago called "diamonds in the rough." Generally, we were first—or second—generation Americans with college educations. We were younger, ambitious, and highly motivated to run a company built on recognizing and appreciating those that did the work because most of us had parents who were blue-collar working-class Americans. Many of our parents were immigrants who came to the US for a better life.

We benefited from the work ethic of our parents and, perhaps subconsciously or consciously, we were driven to be successful, inclusive, and respectful of the 600 people we led. Frankly, the genesis of the philosophy of *The Six Rs* had its roots in the period when the

Faragos ran the business. I can safely say that our team post-1988 took us to the next level and beyond.

Please let me share some of the statistics/benchmarks from NEPTCO:

At a top level, we achieved and sustained profitable growth from 1988 to 2012. We experience two significant downturns in 2001 (the Internet or Dot-com Bubble) and 2008 (Lehman weekend and subsequent financial collapse). In both cases, we rebounded. We never lost money; we recovered, all due to the collective efforts of our team.

Under Cookson PLC (a $2 bil company with approximately 50 reporting businesses) we were named "Company of the Year." The company chosen to be recognized was determined by a number of financial and quality metrics. NEPTCO Inc. was named company of the year once and finished in the top five every year for the 12 years that they owned us.

The wire and cable industry recognized Mr. Peter Farago and me as recipients of its Distinguished Career Award[4], an individual award, but one that generally recognizes those that lead a successful, respected business in its served market.

---

4   Kudos to James Scott George, the 3rd NEPTCO recipient of the Charles Scott Distinguished Career Award. Jim was a senior leader in marketing and sales.

Some notable results:

- Every two years NEPTCO hired an outside, independent firm that prepared a blind customer survey.

- During the time period of 1988 through 2012, customers preferred to buy from NEPTCO over competitors in each of our served markets in every single survey.

- After successful implementation of the company-wide quality improvement system, our metrics showed annual reductions in customer complaints, product returns, scrap, and downtime. Through this process, our costs were reduced dramatically and we were able to gain significant market share. This was the result of the entire team working together with the philosophy of *The Six Rs* as our guiding values.

- Productivity: Every year brought improvement in sales and profits per employee

- Average length of employment for hourly workers and the management team: 20 plus years of seniority.

This last point is an important one, as it reflects the success of *The Six Rs*.

People stayed with us because they were respected, made responsible, recognized, and rewarded. They reciprocated by doing more than what was expected and we developed deep and lasting relationships.

One last point here:

Customers can come and go.
Suppliers and service providers can come and go.
Ownership, investors, and banks can come and go.

Your people, if properly engaged, will get you through the ups and downs.

Chapter 12: Final Thoughts

ONE OF THE REASONS I wrote this book was to pay tribute to the employees of NEPTCO from the period of 1982 – 2012. It was an amazing run for all of us.

Secondly, I truly believe in the principles of *The Six Rs*. The beliefs and methods briefly discussed herein will play a significant role in your company achieving sustainable profitable growth while driving increasing employee engagement. It just makes sense—respect your people, make them responsible for their jobs, recognize and reward them and watch your company's performance improve.

Finally, with respect to income inequality, something needs to be done and it needs to be led by the business community. Some companies treat their employees very well. I was delighted to see Walmart announce that they will support employees who seek higher education through its Live Better in Education Program.

In this book, I shared an example of one way to reduce income inequality. I suggested an "Income Inequality Bonus." I used that term to be provocative; clearly you wouldn't call it that. Call it whatever you like—sharing some of your company's earned income growth with your employees who deliver day in and day out must be considered and ultimately implemented in some fashion.

My parents came to this wonderful country after World War II devastated their Italian homeland. They had an opportunity to participate in the American Experience, or Dream. They were able to improve their lot in life from where they came from and where they started from when they first arrived to the US; they experienced upward mobility. While the love of their native homeland continued, they respected and loved this country; and it became the place they called home.

My parents arrived in the mid-1950s and built a better life up to and through their retirement years. Does our economic system provide the same opportunity today? I believe it does but the opportunity to achieve that better life seems diminished.

Our culture has always provided upward mobility to those who work hard. We need to continue what I and many believe America promises. I don't have all the answers but I do know that Corporate America and business leaders of certain sized companies can lead the way.

Thank you for taking the time to read this and consider these thoughts.

—*Guy Marini*

Acknowledgments

A special thanks to Lois Josephs Kilsey, an innovator and driver in development of *The Six Rs* at NEPTCO

I want to recognize the team:

Dave McWhinnie
  (*deceased*)
Ken Feroldi
Joel Gruhn
Frank Conti
Ashok Gordhandes
Richard Pond
Al Grimshaw
Mark Canrobert
Randy Dula
Ethan Franklin
Rick Copp
Jim George

Thomas Herman
George Shanahan
Ken Dalton
Dharman Hensman
Steve O'Meara
Pete Mikucki
Tom Auger
Dave Braun
Bob Hegan
Barbara Cioffi

And . . .

So many others . . . Thank you.

Finally, thanks to Dr. Timothy Dukes for his valuable guidance and counsel.

About the Author

GUY MARINI IS A FATHER, grandfather (Nonno), and was caregiver to his late wife Mary Lee (M.L.). He graduated from Boston Latin School in 1974 and Boston College in 1978 with a degree in accounting and economics.

He began his business career with Arthur Andersen in Boston and spent 30 years with NEPTCO Inc. serving as president/CEO for 25 of those years. Guy is also the creator of a series of children's books: the Super Nonno books (www.supernonnobooks.com). They are available through major booksellers.